LINCOLN BREWSTER
TODAY IS T...

PIANO / VOCAL / GUITAR

ISBN 978-1-4234-6217-0

7777 W. BLUEMOUND RD. P.O. BOX 13819 MILWAUKEE, WI 53213

For all works contained herein:
Unauthorized copying, arranging, adapting, recording or public performance is an infringement of copyright.
Infringers are liable under the law.

Visit Hal Leonard Online at
www.halleonard.com

4   TODAY IS THE DAY

12 EVERYWHERE I GO

20 GIVE HIM PRAISE

26 GOD YOU REIGN

32 THE ARMS OF MY SAVIOR

37 THIS LOVE

42 THE POWER OF YOUR NAME

59 THE LOVE OF GOD

50 SALVATION IS HERE

64 LET YOUR GLORY SHINE

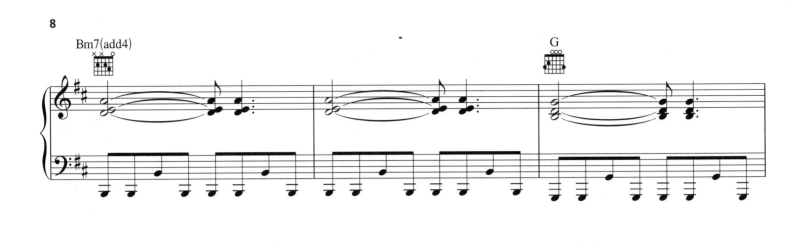
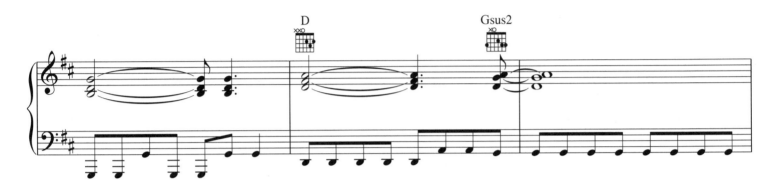
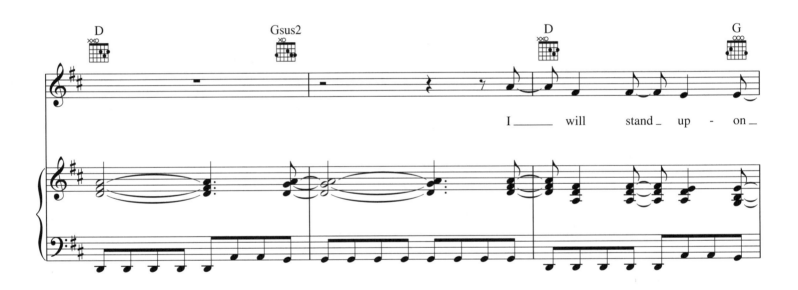
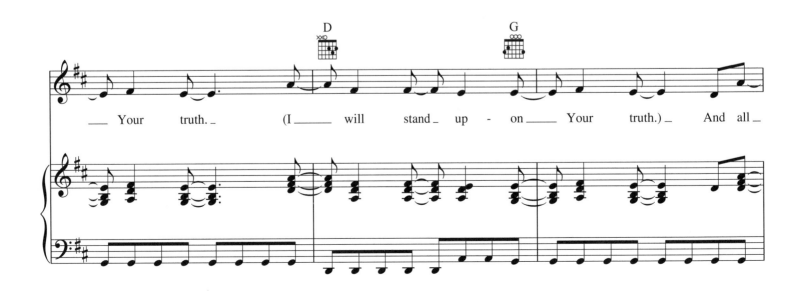

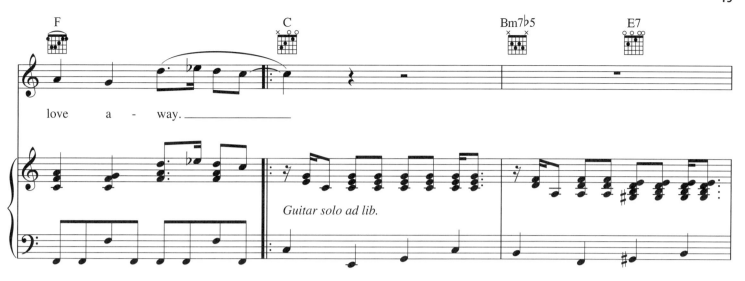
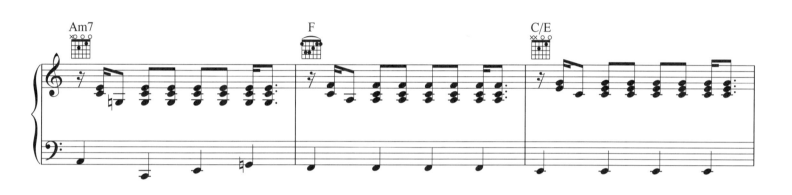
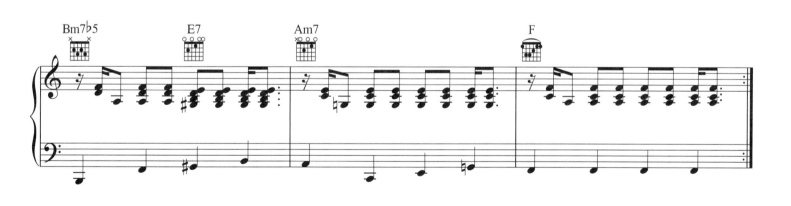

GIVE HIM PRAISE

Words and Music by
LINCOLN BREWSTER

God Al - might - y, we give You praise, __
Psalm nine, verse two and __ one: __

© 2008 Integrity's Praise! Music/BMI
c/o Integrity Media, Inc., 1000 Cody Road, Mobile, AL 36695
All Rights Reserved   International Copyright Secured   Used by Permission

GOD YOU REIGN

Words and Music by LINCOLN BREWSTER
and MIA FIELDES

© 2008 Integrity's Praise! Music/BMI and Mia Fieldes/Hillsong Publishing/ASCAP (admin. by Integrity's Hosanna! Music)
c/o Integrity Media, Inc., 1000 Cody Road, Mobile, AL 36695
All Rights Reserved   International Copyright Secured   Used by Permission

THE ARMS OF MY SAVIOR

Words and Music by
LINCOLN BREWSTER

THIS LOVE

Words and Music by LINCOLN BREWSTER
and MIA FIELDES

Easy Rock

One love to o-ver-shad-ow ev-'ry oth-er love, oth-er love.
One love be-yond the heav-ens and deep-er than the sea, oh, oh.

One love to break the dark-ness,
One love will be for-ev-er

© 2008 Integrity's Praise! Music/BMI and Mia Fieldes/Hillsong Publishing/ASCAP (admin. by Integrity's Hosanna! Music)
c/o Integrity Media, Inc., 1000 Cody Road, Mobile, AL 36695
All Rights Reserved International Copyright Secured Used by Permission

38

THE POWER OF YOUR NAME

Words and Music by LINCOLN BREWSTER and MIA FIELDES

© 2008 Integrity's Praise! Music/BMI and Mia Fieldes/Hillsong Publishing/ASCAP (admin. by Integrity's Hosanna! Music)
c/o Integrity Media, Inc., 1000 Cody Road, Mobile, AL 36695
All Rights Reserved International Copyright Secured Used by Permission

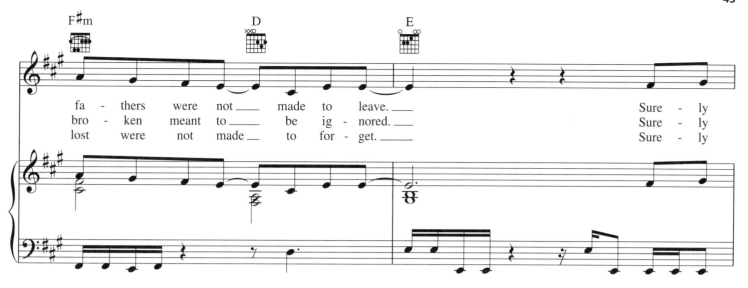

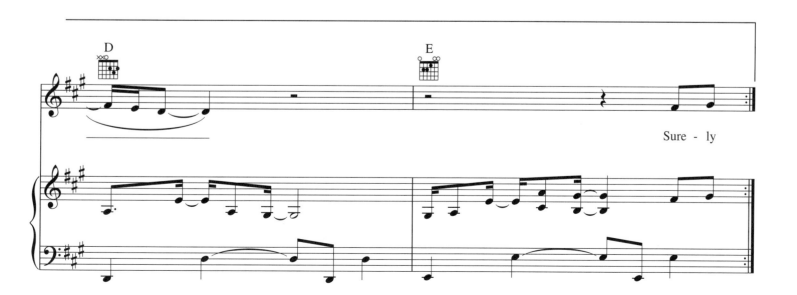

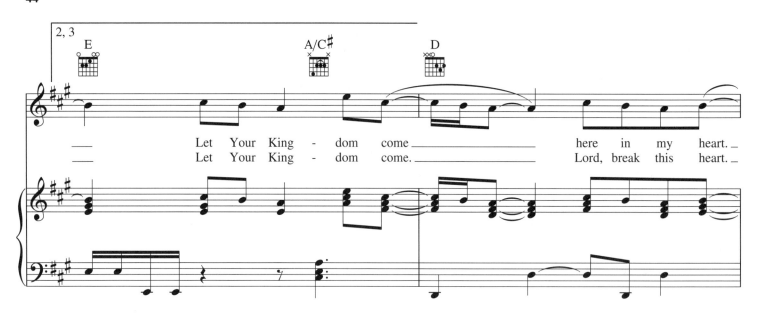
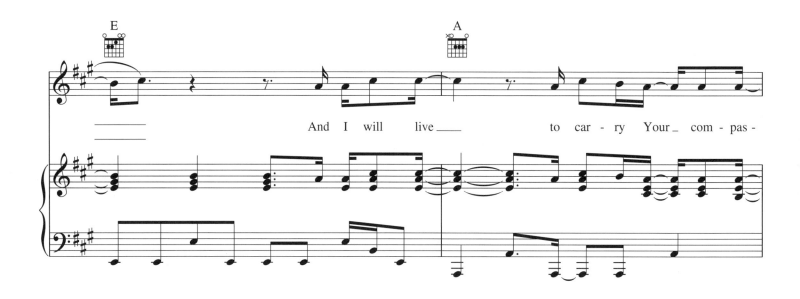
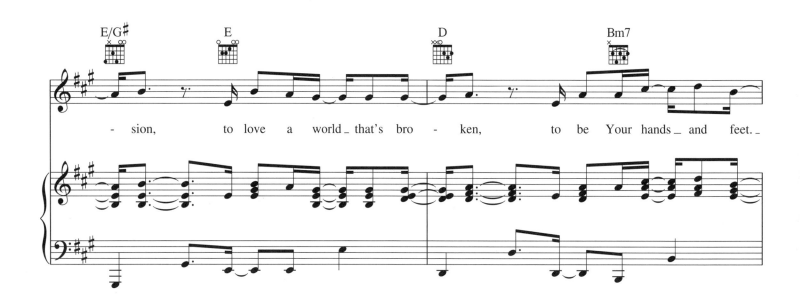

THE LOVE OF GOD

Words and Music by LINCOLN BREWSTER
and MIA FIELDES

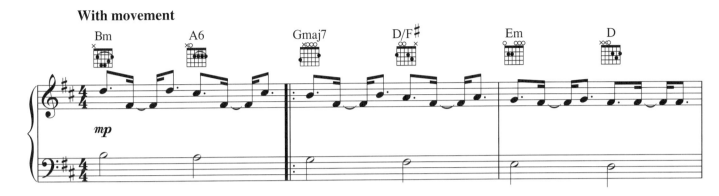
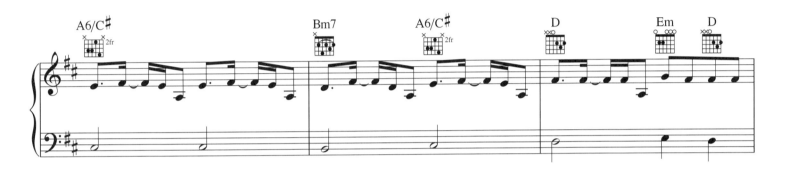
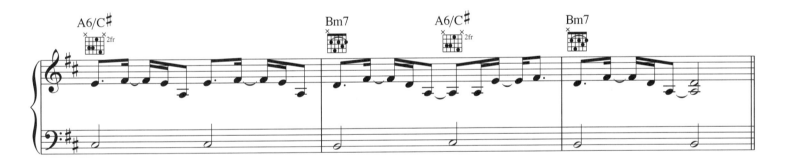
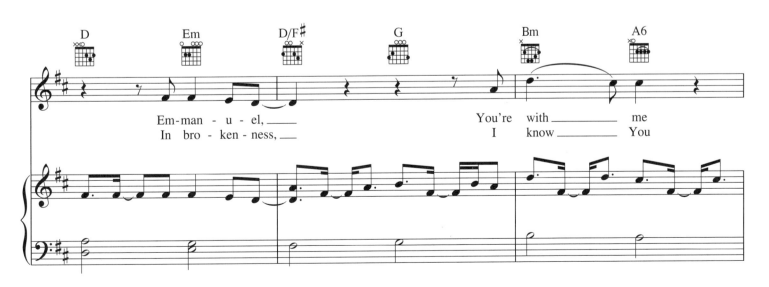

Em-man-u-el, _____ You're with _____ me
In bro-ken-ness, _____ I know _____ You

© 2008 Integrity's Praise! Music/BMI and Mia Fieldes/Hillsong Publishing/ASCAP (admin. by Integrity's Hosanna! Music)
c/o Integrity Media, Inc., 1000 Cody Road, Mobile, AL 36695
All Rights Reserved   International Copyright Secured   Used by Permission

LET YOUR GLORY SHINE

Words and Music by LINCOLN BREWSTER
and MIA FIELDES

Your love won't de-ny__ me, e-ven in the storm You find__ me,
I know You're the Sav - ior, You're tak-ing ev-'ry fear and fail - ure,
You call me from the dark - ness to Your light.___
You're lift-ing me to rise a-bove it all.___

© 2008 Integrity's Praise! Music/BMI and Mia Fieldes/Hillsong Publishing/ASCAP (admin. by Integrity's Hosanna! Music)
c/o Integrity Media, Inc., 1000 Cody Road, Mobile, AL 36695
All Rights Reserved   International Copyright Secured   Used by Permission

THE BEST PRAISE & WORSHIP SONGBOOKS

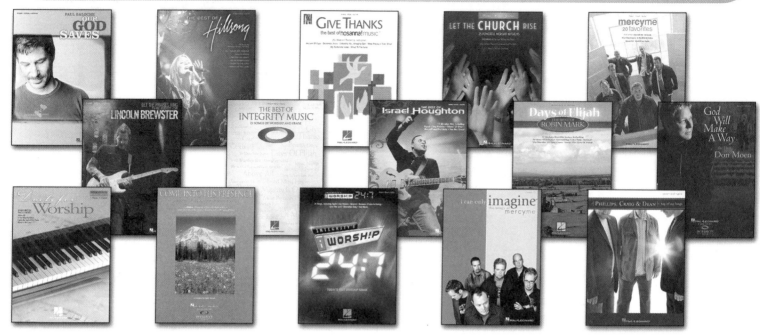

PAUL BALOCHE – OUR GOD SAVES
Matching folio to the live album recorded at his church in Lindale, Texas. 13 songs, including: God Most High • Great Redeemer • Hallelujah to My King • Our God Saves • Praise • Rock of Ages You Will Stand • The Way • Your Love Came Down • and more.
_____00306940 P/V/G........................$16.95

LET THE PRAISES RING – THE BEST OF LINCOLN BREWSTER
Christian guitarist/singer/songwriter Lincoln Brewster was born in Fairbanks, AK but migrated to L.A., Oklahoma, then Nashville for his music making. This folio features Brewster's best, including the hit singles "All to You," "Everlasting God," and 14 more.
_____00306856 P/V/G........................$17.95

DUETS FOR WORSHIP
Intermediate Level • 1 Piano, 4 Hands
8 favorites for worship, including: Above All • I Give You My Heart • Open the Eyes of My Heart • Shout to the Lord • and more.
_____08745730 Piano Duet.............$10.95

THE BEST OF HILLSONG
25 of the most popular songs from Hillsong artists and writers, including: Blessed • Eagle's Wings • God Is Great • The Potter's Hand • Shout to the Lord • Worthy Is the Lamb • You Are Near • and more.
_____08739789 P/V/G........................$16.95

THE BEST OF INTEGRITY MUSIC
25 of the best praise & worship songs from Integrity: Ancient of Days • Celebrate Jesus • Firm Foundation • Give Thanks • Mighty Is Our God • Open the Eyes of My Heart • Trading My Sorrows • You Are Good • and more.
_____08739790 P/V/G........................$16.95

COME INTO HIS PRESENCE
Features 12 beautiful piano solo arrangements of worship favorites: Above All • Blessed Be the Lord God Almighty • Breathe • Come Into His Presence • Draw Me Close • Give Thanks • God Will Make a Way • Jesus, Name Above All Names/Blessed Be the Name of the Lord • Lord Have Mercy • More Precious Than Silver • Open the Eyes of My Heart • Shout to the Lord.
_____08739299 Piano Solo.............$12.95

GIVE THANKS – THE BEST OF HOSANNA! MUSIC
This superb best-of collection features 25 worship favorites published by Hosanna! Music: Ancient of Days • Celebrate Jesus • I Worship You, Almighty God • More Precious Than Silver • My Redeemer Lives • Shout to the Lord • and more.
08739729 P/V/G........................$14.95
08739745 Easy Piano..................$12.95

THE BEST OF ISRAEL HOUGHTON
13 songs from the Grammy®- and multiple Dove Award-winning worship leader including his work with New Breed and Lakewood Church. Songs include: Again I Say Rejoice • Friend of God • I Lift up My Hands • Magnificent and Holy • Sweeter • Turn It Around • more.
_____00306925 P/V/G........................$16.95

iWORSHIP 24:7 SONGBOOK
This album-matching folio features favorite worship songs by top artists, including: Again I Say Rejoice • Amazed • Hosanna (Praise Is Rising) • Love the Lord • Revelation Song • Your Name • and more.
_____00311466 P/V/G........................$17.95

LET THE CHURCH RISE
25 Powerful Worship Anthems
This collection features: All the Earth Will Sing Your Praises • Days of Elijah • Hear Us from Heaven • Lord Most High • Shout to the Lord • Your Name • and more.
_____00311435 P/V/G........................$14.95

For More Information, See Your Local Music Dealer, Or Write To:

HAL•LEONARD® CORPORATION
7777 W. BLUEMOUND RD. P.O. BOX 13819
MILWAUKEE, WISCONSIN 53213
Complete song lists available online at
www.halleonard.com

DAYS OF ELIJAH – THE BEST OF ROBIN MARK
Robin Mark's worship music blends traditional Irish instrumentation with the passion of modern worship. This compilation features 14 songs: Ancient Words • Days of Elijah • Lord Have Mercy • Revival • Shout to the North • and more.
_____00306944 P/V/G........................$16.95

THE SONGS OF MERCYME – I CAN ONLY IMAGINE
10 of the most recognizable songs from this popular Contemporary Christian group, including the smash hit "I Can Only Imagine," plus: Cannot Say Enough • Here with Me • Homesick • How Great Is Your Love • The Love of God • Spoken For • Unaware • Where You Lead Me • Word of God Speak.
_____08739803 Piano Solo.............$12.95

MERCYME – 20 FAVORITES
A jam-packed collection of 20 of their best. Includes: Crazy • Go • Here with Me • I Can Only Imagine • In the Blink of an Eye • Never Alone • On My Way to You • Spoken For • Undone • Word of God Speak • Your Glory Goes On • and more.
_____08739862 P/V/G........................$17.95

THE BEST OF DON MOEN – GOD WILL MAKE A WAY
19 of the greatest hits from this Dove Award-winning singer/songwriter. Includes: Celebrate Jesus • God Will Make a Way • Here We Are • I Will Sing • Let Your Glory Fall • Shout to the Lord • We Give You Glory • You Make Me Lie down in Green Pastures • and more.
_____08739297 P/V/G........................$16.95

PHILLIPS, CRAIG & DEAN – TOP OF MY LUNGS
Our matching folio to the 2006 release by this popular CCM trio of full-time pastors includes the hit single "Your Name," the title song, and eight more: Amazed • Because of That Blood • I Will Boast • One Way • That's My Lord • more.
_____08745913 P/V/G........................$16.95

Prices, contents, & availability subject to change without notice.